DISCOVER WHAT'S INSIDE

KU-714-773

02 Let's Get Started

04 Deadly Mammals

16 Activities

18 Deadly Sea Creatures

30 Activities

32 Deadly Reptiles and Amphibians

44 Activities

46 Deadly Spiders and Insects

58 Activities

60 Deadly Winged Creatures

72 Activities

74 Answers

77 Glossary

LET'S GET STARTED

Get ready to meet some of the most deadly creatures on the planet! This book will introduce you to some truly terrifying animals. Some are predators that hunt and kill other animals for food, using super-sharp teeth or claws (called carnivores). Some are plant-eaters (called herbivores), but they are no less dangerous. They can possess impressive weapons and they are not afraid to defend themselves against attackers.

All the animals in this book have been given points based on the following categories:

- 🐾 **fearsome facts**
- 🐾 **grisly tactics**
- 🐾 **awesome weapons**

The points are added up to find out each animal's total score.

Abbreviation chart:

ft = feet
in = inches

lb = pounds
mph = miles per hour

oz = ounces

FEARSOME FACTS

This category looks at the statistics of each creature, such as size, strength, or camouflage ability. What are the things that rank it alongside the deadliest creatures on the planet?

GRISLY TACTICS

All these deadly creatures have different ways of catching their prey. Points are awarded here for the methods each creature has developed, including skill, ingenuity, intelligence or an element of surprise.

AWESOME WEAPONS

Teeth, claws, poison, or the power to leap, ambush or run fast. All of these creatures have abilities that make them the stuff of nightmares.

DEADLY SCORE

Add these up and you have an overall deadly score for each of these amazing creatures. Turn the pages to find out more...

FEARSOME FACTS: 6/10

GRISLY TACTICS: 5/10

AWESOME WEAPONS: 6/10

DEADLY SCORE: 17/30

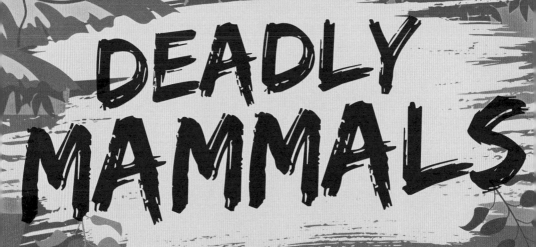

DEADLY
MAMMALS

A mammal is a warm-blooded animal that feeds its young with milk it produces. Doesn't sound too scary? Some of the fiercest animals on the planet are included in this category, with killer teeth, claws or just sheer size to hunt for food, protect their territory or defend their young.

DINGO

(Scientific name: Canis lupus dingo)

Eats: rabbits and rodents, eggs, birds, carrion, fruit and nuts

Dingoes might look like friendly dogs, but they are definitely not pets. They are the largest land predators in Australia and are more wolf than dog.

DEADLY POINTS

FEARSOME FACTS: 5/10

GRISLY TACTICS: 5/10

AWESOME WEAPONS: 6/10

DEADLY SCORE: 16/30

APEX PREDATORS THAT ARE PERFECTLY ADAPTED TO THEIR HABITAT

FEARSOME FACTS

Dingoes are medium-sized carnivores, with an average body length of 1.2 metres (4 ft). They weigh around 13–23 kilograms (29–51 lbs). Dingoes are flexible and agile so they can squeeze through very small gaps, and have special rotating wrists that allow them to climb trees.

GRISLY TACTICS

The harsh, dry conditions of Australia are no problem for this tough predator. Dingoes are tireless and can travel up to 40 kilometres (25 miles) in one day in search of food. Working in packs they can bring down animals much bigger than themselves such as kangaroos.

AWESOME WEAPONS

With great hearing and eyesight, strong jaws and large sharp teeth, dingoes are designed for hunting. Reaching speeds of 48 kilometres per hour (30 mph) they can chase their prey to exhaustion before moving in for the kill.

DEADLY POINTS

FEARSOME FACTS: 5/10

GRISLY TACTICS: 6/10

AWESOME WEAPONS: 6/10

DEADLY SCORE: 17/30

SMALL BUT FEROCIOUS HUNTERS THAT PREY ON LEMURS

FOSSA

(Scientific name: Cryptoprocta ferox)

Eats: mainly lemurs, but also birds, mice, fish and small mammals

The largest predator native to Madagascar, the cat-like fossa lives in remote forested areas and is a fierce and highly successful hunter.

FEARSOME FACTS

Fossae are slender with small heads and rounded ears. They measure around 70–80 centimetres (27.5–31 in) head to tail, with tails of 65–70 centimetres (25.5–27.5 in). They weigh around 5.5–8.6 kilograms (12.1–18.9 lbs). They may be small, but they are definitely deadly!

GRISLY TACTICS

Fossae are equally at home on the ground or in trees. Their dark coats provide camouflage as they stalk their prey at night through the branches before pouncing at incredible speed. The final act is to dispatch their victim with razor-sharp teeth and claws.

AWESOME WEAPONS

Fossae have semi-retractable claws and flexible ankles to help them climb easily through the trees, using their long slender tails for balance. Their large footpads help keep them stable and provide balance as they leap from branch to branch.

WOLVERINE

(Scientific name: Gulo gulo)

Eats: carrion, deer, rabbits and small mammals, rodents, eggs and berries

DEADLY POINTS

FEARSOME FACTS: 6/10
GRISLY TACTICS: 5/10
AWESOME WEAPONS: 7/10
DEADLY SCORE: 18/30

A POWERFUL PREDATOR WITH A REPUTATION FOR FEROCITY AND CUNNING

Looking rather like a small bear, the wolverine is a ferocious predator that can kill prey much larger than itself.

FEARSOME FACTS

The wolverine is a stocky muscular animal with short legs ending in large five-toed paws. It measures around 65–100 centimetres (25.5–39 in), with a bushy tail of around 15–26 centimetres (5.9–10 in), and a typical weight of 9–27 kilograms (20–60 lbs).

GRISLY TACTICS

Wolverines are opportunistic scavengers, eating carrion and sometimes even taking food from other predators. They are fearless hunters as well, and will attack pretty much any animal they meet, using ambushes and speed to take down even the biggest prey.

KILLER FACT

WOLVERINES HAVE BEEN KNOWN TO KILL MOOSE TWENTY TIMES THEIR SIZE.

AWESOME WEAPONS

As well as its sheer strength, the wolverine has powerful bone-cracking jaws with rotated teeth that can bite through frozen meat. Its large flat feet help it move through deep snow and are tipped with razor-sharp curved claws to grab on to its prey.

WILD BOAR

(Scientific name: Sus scrofa)

Eats: a wide range of food including plants, roots, berries, nuts, seeds, small insects, worms and small mammals

An aggressive, powerful and intelligent animal with fearsomely sharp tusks.

FEARSOME FACTS

Wild boars are large, standing up to 80 centimetres (31 in) high and weighing between 60–100 kilograms (132–220 lbs). Their huge heads are up to a third of their body length and they have powerful neck muscles that make them well-suited for digging out food.

GRISLY TACTICS

Wild boars are nocturnal and naturally shy, but if they feel threatened are extremely dangerous. They can run fast, at speeds of up to 40 kilometres per hour (25 mph), and will repeatedly charge at an attacker, slashing and stabbing with their razor-sharp tusks.

KILLER FACT

IN ANCIENT CULTURES, KILLING A BOAR PROVED A WARRIOR'S STRENGTH AND BRAVERY.

AWESOME WEAPONS

The wild boar's main weapon is its sharp and deadly tusks, and its sheer bulk and thick hide provide a good defence against predators. Although its eyesight is poor, it has a very good sense of smell which is used to locate food and detect danger.

DEADLY POINTS

FEARSOME FACTS: 6/10

GRISLY TACTICS: 5/10

AWESOME WEAPONS: 8/10

DEADLY SCORE: 19/30

A STOCKY, POWERFUL ANIMAL WITH FEARSOME TUSKS

CHEETAH

(Scientific name: Acinonyx jubatus)

Eats: medium-sized prey such as gazelle, antelope and impala

The fastest land animal, capable of speeds of up to 112 kilometres per hour (70 mph).

DEADLY POINTS

FEARSOME FACTS: 5/10

GRISLY TACTICS: 6/10

AWESOME WEAPONS: 9/10

DEADLY SCORE: 20/30

A LEAN AND DEADLY HUNTING MACHINE

FEARSOME FACTS

Cheetahs are large cats, built for speed with relatively long legs and a lean body. They measure around 0.9–1.2 metres (3–4 ft) long, with a tail length of around 63–81 centimetres (25–32 in). They weigh around 35–65 kilograms (77–143 lbs).

GRISLY TACTICS

Cheetahs stalk their prey, using the long grass of the plains for cover and conserving their energy until the last minute. When they are close enough, they begin the final sprint, zig-zagging as they go, until they get close enough to bring their target down.

AWESOME WEAPONS

Enlarged nostrils, heart and lungs enable the cheetah to sprint very fast. Its long tail helps it steer and keep its balance during the chase. Its deadly claws are semi-retractable and grip the ground as it runs, and it dispatches its victim with sharp teeth.

COUGAR

(Scientific name: Puma concolor)

Eats: any meat it can get, including insects, raccoons, mountain goats and deer

Known also as the mountain lion, the cougar is a secretive and stealthy predator native to the Americas.

FEARSOME FACTS

Cougars are more closely related to domestic cats than to big cats. They vary in size, but on average are around 1.5–2.4 metres (5–8 ft), with tails of 63–89 centimetres (25–35 in), and weigh between 25–150 kilograms (55–330 lbs).

GRISLY TACTICS

Cougars are solitary ambush hunters and stalk their prey using rocks, plants and trees as cover. Their exceptionally powerful hind legs allow them to sprint and leap on to their victim before killing it with a suffocating bite to the neck.

AWESOME WEAPONS

With a light skeleton combined with powerful muscles, cougars are extremely agile and can swim, climb and sprint at speeds of up to 80 kilometres per hour (50 mph). Large front paws grip their prey with five deadly claws so there is no escape.

KILLER FACT

COUGARS CAN LEAP VERTICALLY IN THE AIR UP TO 5 METRES (16 FT).

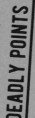

AFRICAN ELEPHANT

(Scientific name: Loxodonta africana)

Eats: grass, leaves, tree branches, bark and fruit

A highly intelligent herbivore, the gigantic African elephant is deadly when agitated.

FEARSOME FACTS

The largest land animals on Earth, African elephants are around 4 metres (13 ft) tall and weigh 6 tonnes (13,000 lbs). Their impressive tusks, which are elongated incisor teeth, can be as long as 3 metres (10 ft). Elephants can live for around seventy years.

GRISLY TACTICS

Elephants are unpredictable and can become extremely aggressive if they feel threatened. They have been known to flip safari jeeps, snap trees in half and confront black rhinos. Their excellent memories mean they can sometimes attack purely for revenge.

KILLER FACT

HUNDREDS OF HUMANS ARE KILLED BY ELEPHANT ATTACKS EACH YEAR.

AWESOME WEAPONS

The enormous size of an elephant means it can simply crush or kick its victims to death, using its massive feet as weapons. Its killer tusks can tear through flesh and bone, and it can lash out with its incredibly strong trunk.

WEASEL

(Scientific name: Mustela nivalis)

Eats: small mammals, rabbits and birds

The smallest carnivores on the planet, weasels may look cute, but they are bloodthirsty killers.

FEARSOME FACTS

Weasels have a body length of a mere 17–22 centimetres (7–9 in), with a tail measuring around 3–5 centimetres (1.2–2 in). They weigh around 55–130 grams (0.1–0.3 lbs), and have very fast metabolisms, meaning they need to eat around a third of their bodyweight each day.

GRISLY TACTICS

Weasels are ruthless killers and do not hesitate to take on animals or birds many times their size. They wrap their flexible bodies around their prey before biting at their throats or through their skulls. These ferocious creatures do a "death dance" to hypnotize and terrify their victim.

KILLER FACT

WEASELS CLIMB TREES TO STEAL EGGS OR TO EAT BABY BIRDS.

AWESOME WEAPONS

Weasels have long slender bodies for pursuing prey through underground burrows, and they move at the speed of lightning. They have excellent night vision, powerful jaws and teeth, and five sharp claws on each foot. To defend themselves they can release a blast of stinky fluid!

DEADLY POINTS

FEARSOME FACTS: 8/10

GRISLY TACTICS: 10/10

AWESOME WEAPONS: 7/10

DEADLY SCORE: 25/30

TINY AND VILLAINOUS ASSASSINS

HIPPO

(Scientific name: Hippopotamus amphibius)

Eats: grass, fruit and other vegetation

Hippos may look sleepy and relaxed as they wallow in rivers, but they are one of the most dangerous land animals in Africa.

DEADLY POINTS

FEARSOME FACTS: 9/10

GRISLY TACTICS: 10/10

AWESOME WEAPONS: 8/10

DEADLY SCORE: 27/30

UNPREDICTABLE AND AGGRESSIVE GIANTS

FEARSOME FACTS

Hippos can grow to 5 metres (16 ft) long and stand 1.6 metres (5.2 ft) tall. They can weigh up to 3.5 tonnes (7,710 lbs). Hippos spend most of their time in water to keep cool, and can stay submerged for up to five minutes before surfacing to catch their victims off-guard.

GRISLY TACTICS

Male hippos are extremely territorial, while females are protective of their young. When hippos become aggressive, nothing can stand in their way. They can charge at an impressive 48 kilometres per hour (30 mph) and have been known to attack boats and tip them over.

AWESOME WEAPONS

Hippos have huge, self-sharpening teeth and canines resembling tusks that can measure 50 centimetres (20 in) in length. Their massive jaws open to 180 degrees to inflict a mighty bite that can crush a crocodile. Their huge bulk deters other predators from attacking them.

KILLER FACT

ALTHOUGH THEY ARE HERBIVORES, HIPPOS HAVE BEEN KNOWN TO EAT THE CARCASSES OF ANIMALS, INCLUDING OTHER HIPPOS.

JAGUAR

(Scientific name: Panthera onca)

Eats: anything they can catch, including snakes, deer, monkeys and tapirs

Apex predators of their habitat, jaguars are opportunistic hunters feeding only on meat and fish.

Did you know?

Unlike other big cats, jaguars love water and will hunt fish, turtles and even crocodiles.

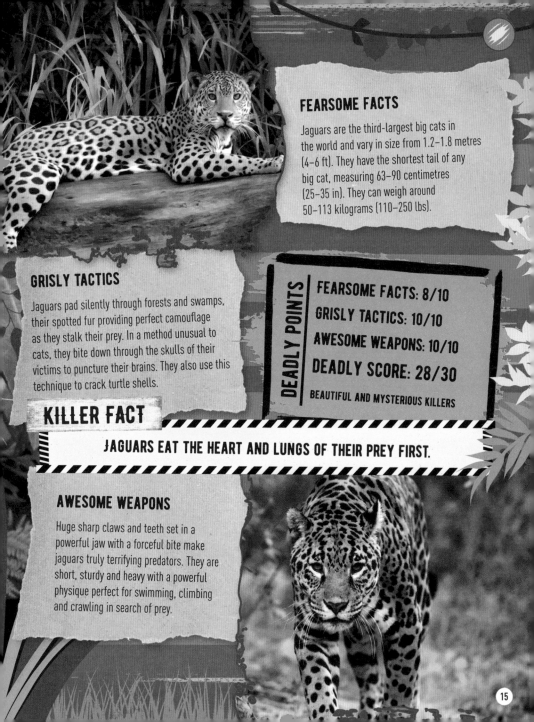

FEARSOME FACTS

Jaguars are the third-largest big cats in the world and vary in size from 1.2–1.8 metres (4–6 ft). They have the shortest tail of any big cat, measuring 63–90 centimetres (25–35 in). They can weigh around 50–113 kilograms (110–250 lbs).

GRISLY TACTICS

Jaguars pad silently through forests and swamps, their spotted fur providing perfect camouflage as they stalk their prey. In a method unusual to cats, they bite down through the skulls of their victims to puncture their brains. They also use this technique to crack turtle shells.

DEADLY POINTS

FEARSOME FACTS: 8/10
GRISLY TACTICS: 10/10
AWESOME WEAPONS: 10/10
DEADLY SCORE: 28/30

BEAUTIFUL AND MYSTERIOUS KILLERS

KILLER FACT

JAGUARS EAT THE HEART AND LUNGS OF THEIR PREY FIRST.

AWESOME WEAPONS

Huge sharp claws and teeth set in a powerful jaw with a forceful bite make jaguars truly terrifying predators. They are short, sturdy and heavy with a powerful physique perfect for swimming, climbing and crawling in search of prey.

```
O C K V H I J O E B M O
X E O W U A Q N P C U C
W L N U G H I K L P I W
E A Z U G R S Z G X I N
A B A R E A W A L A F H
S R R V U J R R J S O W
E X L R Y W P R X S J L
L O C H E E T A H O S L
W O G N I D Y X O F I J
Q U U U P O O O E H J L
U X K S F I E P D X O H
T M F S Q J Z A D A Y W
```

Can you find these eight words hidden in the grid above?

DINGO • FOSSA • WOLVERINE • CHEETAH

HIPPO • COUGAR • WEASEL • JAGUAR

TEST YOUR KNOWLEDGE!

Now that you've read all about these terrifying mammals, can you answer these questions?

1. Where do fossae live?

   a. open grassland b. remote forested areas c. deserts

2. What do weasels do to defend themselves?

   a. make a loud hissing sound
   b. stiffen their tails to make themselves look more intimidating
   c. release a blast of stinky fluid

3. What do the special rotating wrists of dingoes allow them to do?

   a. climb trees
   b. run fast
   c. bring down prey bigger than themselves

4. How fast can a hippo charge?

   a. 20 kilometres per hour (12.4 mph)
   b. 48 kilometres per hour (30 mph)
   c. 63 kilometres per hour (39 mph)

5. What do the enlarged nostrils, heart and lungs of cheetahs allow them to do?

   a. survive in extremely hot conditions
   b. live at high altitudes
   c. sprint fast

Answers on page 74

DEADLY SEA CREATURES

In the oceans of our planet there live some of the world's most terrifying predators. They come in an amazing array of sizes and shapes, from monstrous giant crabs to beautiful but deadly starfish. Giant sharks actively hunt near the surface while bizarre-looking ambush hunters lurk deep in the dark depths of the ocean.

JAPANESE SPIDER CRAB

(Scientific name: Macrocheira kaempferi)

Eats: clams, mussels, kelp and carrion

The stuff of nightmares, the giant Japanese spider crab is a terrifying sight as it lurks on the ocean floor.

FEARSOME FACTS

Japanese spider crabs are the largest crabs in the world. Although their bodies only measure around 38 centimetres (15 in), they have a truly impressive leg span of up to 4 metres (13 ft). They can weigh up to 20 kilograms (44 lbs).

DEADLY POINTS

FEARSOME FACTS: 6/10

GRISLY TACTICS: 5/10

AWESOME WEAPONS: 6/10

DEADLY SCORE: 17/30

SHARP-CLAWED KILLER AND SCAVENGER

KILLER FACT

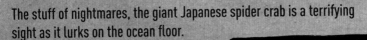

THESE CREEPY GIANTS HAVE THE LONGEST LIFESPAN OF ANY CRAB AND CAN LIVE FOR 100 YEARS!

GRISLY TACTICS

Japanese spider crabs eat any plants or animals they can find, including algae, molluscs and invertebrates. However, they prefer to scavenge dead and decaying bodies than to hunt. Young crabs decorate their shells to disguise themselves and protect against predators.

AWESOME WEAPONS

These fearsome crabs have sharp claws on the end of muscly legs, perfect for killing smaller prey and for opening up shells to get at the meat inside. Their legs are weak and often break off, however, the crab can survive with up to three legs missing.

GIANT MORAY EEL

(Scientific name: Gymnothorax javanicus)

Eats: fish, molluscs and crustaceans

DEADLY POINTS

FEARSOME FACTS: 7/10

GRISLY TACTICS: 6/10

AWESOME WEAPONS: 5/10

DEADLY SCORE: 18/30

A STEALTHY AND SLIPPERY PREDATOR

A powerful, active predator that lurks in caves by day and hunts by night.

FEARSOME FACTS

Giant morays can reach up to 2.5 metres (8 ft) in length and weigh around 30 kilograms (66 lbs). They are found in tropical lagoons and coral reefs where they hide in crevices or under ledges during the day.

KILLER FACT

MORAY EELS ARE DANGEROUS TO EAT DUE TO THE TOXINS IN THEIR BODIES.

GRISLY TACTICS

At night the moray eel hunts for prey using its excellent sense of smell. It is one of the few creatures on the planet that hunts with another species, in this case grouper fish, which cover the open water while the eel slides in to flush out the prey.

AWESOME WEAPONS

The giant moray's strong jaws contain large, sharp teeth that can rip flesh and grab slippery prey. Once the prey is trapped the eel uses a second set of jaws in its throat to pull it in and swallow it.

DEADLY POINTS

FEARSOME FACTS: 5/10

GRISLY TACTICS : 6/10

AWESOME WEAPONS: 8/10

DEADLY SCORE: 19/30

BEAUTIFUL BUT DEADLY AMBUSH HUNTER

SEA ANEMONE

(Scientific name: Actiniaria spp.)

Eats: fish, mussels, plankton and worms

A sea creature that looks like an ornate flower but is armed with deadly weapons to subdue its prey.

FEARSOME FACTS

There are around 1,000 types of sea anemone around the world. They range in size from the tiny, rare *Gonactina prolifera* which only reaches 5 millimetres (0.2 in) tall, to tropical species measuring as much as 1.8 metres (6 ft) across.

GRISLY TACTICS

Sea anemones anchor themselves with their adhesive feet and wait for prey to swim past. They extend their tentacles and inject their victim with venom to immobilize it. Once the prey is paralysed, it can be guided into their mouths.

AWESOME WEAPONS

Anemones' mouths are in the centre of their bodies, surrounded by venom-laden tentacles, and can be opened wide to swallow some prey whole. The stinging cells on their tentacles are triggered by touch and are used to paralyse prey and also to defend against attackers.

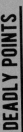

FEARSOME FACTS: 7/10

GRISLY TACTICS: 7/10

AWESOME WEAPONS: 7/10

DEADLY SCORE: 21/30

A GRUESOME AND GREEDY STARFISH

CROWN-OF-THORNS
STARFISH

(Scientific name: Acanthaster planci)

Eats: coral polyps

7

The only venomous starfish, the crown-of-thorns starfish has toxic spines and a killer digestive system.

FEARSOME FACTS

One of the largest starfish in the world, the crown-of-thorns starfish can grow up to 1 metre (3 ft) wide. It has a central disk and up to twenty-one arms. Its body is covered in long, sharp spikes around 6 centimetres (2 in) long.

GRISLY TACTICS

To eat, the starfish turns its stomach inside out so that its digestive juices can liquefy the coral on which it feeds. These starfish are voracious eaters, killing more than their own body width of coral each day, and causing great damage to coral reefs.

KILLER FACT

CROWN-OF-THORNS STARFISH ARE ONE OF THE BIGGEST THREATS TO THE GREAT BARRIER REEF IN AUSTRALIA.

AWESOME WEAPONS

This starfish uses its spines for defence. Not only are they sharp, but they contain toxins to deter predators. The spines can break off and become embedded in an attacker. In humans, they cause painful swelling and sickness.

PUFFERFISH

(Scientific name: Tetraodontidae spp.)

Eats: algae and small invertebrates

One of the most poisonous creatures on the planet, pufferfish contain a toxin deadlier than cyanide.

FEARSOME FACTS

There are around 100 species of pufferfish worldwide. They vary in appearance and size, with the largest reaching around 90 centimetres (35 in) in length. They have tough, spiky skin, and beak-like teeth with which they can crush molluscs and crustaceans.

DEADLY POINTS

FEARSOME FACTS: 5/10

GRISLY TACTICS: 7/10

AWESOME WEAPONS: 10/10

DEADLY SCORE: 22/30

A DEADLY SPIKY BALL LOADED WITH VENOM

GRISLY TACTICS

The pufferfish has excellent eyesight and can swim fast to escape predators, but if that doesn't work, it fills its stomach with water or air and inflates itself into a spiky ball. The predator may retreat, or choke on its catch.

AWESOME WEAPONS

Pufferfish use their toxin to deter or even kill predators. The venom, tetrodotoxin (TTX), is fatal to humans. Symptoms begin with numbness and sickness, followed by paralysis and death within hours. There is no known antidote.

ANGLERFISH

(Scientific name: Lophiiformes spp.)

Eats: a wide range of fish of all sizes

These bizarre-looking fish live in one of the most inhospitable habitats of all – the freezing, dark bottom of the ocean.

DEADLY POINTS

FEARSOME FACTS: 6/10

GRISLY TACTICS: 8/10

AWESOME WEAPONS: 9/10

DEADLY SCORE: 23/30

GROTESQUE DEEP-SEA AMBUSH HUNTERS

FEARSOME FACTS

Anglerfish range in size from 20 centimetres (8 in) to over 1 metre (3.2 ft) long, and weigh up to 45 kilograms (99 lbs). The females have a dorsal spine protruding above their mouths, with a luminescent organ, called an esca, at the end. It is used as bait when hunting.

GRISLY TACTICS

Female anglerfish drift slowly along, dangling their luminous escas, that look like worms, to attract prey. Once close enough, they use suction to drag their victims in. The males do not have lures, they survive by permanently attaching themselves to the females.

AWESOME WEAPONS

Anglerfish have enormous, crescent-shaped mouths full of dagger-sharp teeth that are angled inwards to grab prey, and can be lowered so they can swallow more easily. Their jaws and stomachs can expand so that they can swallow prey twice their size.

DEADLY POINTS

FEARSOME FACTS: 8/10

GRISLY TACTICS: 7/10

AWESOME WEAPONS: 9/10

DEADLY SCORE: 24/30

AN AGGRESSIVE, FEARLESS AND TERRIFYING SHARK

TIGER SHARK

(Scientific name: Galeocerdo cuvier)

Eats: seals, turtles, fish, birds, sea snakes and rubbish

FEARSOME FACTS

The tiger shark is the second-largest predatory shark at around 3–4 metres (10–13 ft), weighing around 380–640 kilograms (838–1,410 lbs). It has a blue-green back and a pale underside, so it is camouflaged in the water from above and below.

Known as the "dustbin of the ocean", this ferocious shark will eat pretty much anything.

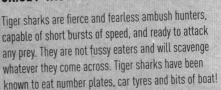

GRISLY TACTICS

Tiger sharks are fierce and fearless ambush hunters, capable of short bursts of speed, and ready to attack any prey. They are not fussy eaters and will scavenge whatever they come across. Tiger sharks have been known to eat number plates, car tyres and bits of boat!

AWESOME WEAPONS

The large, distinctive teeth of the tiger shark make it a truly deadly predator. The main part of the tooth has a razor-sharp point for ripping open prey, and along the edge are smaller notches that are ideal for sawing up food. Tiger sharks can crack the tough shells of sea turtles.

KILLER FACT

THE TIGER SHARK IS ONE OF THE "BIG THREE" MOST DEADLY SHARKS, WITH THE BULL SHARK AND THE GREAT WHITE.

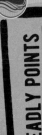

DEADLY POINTS

FEARSOME FACTS: 8/10

GRISLY TACTICS: 8/10

AWESOME WEAPONS: 9/10

DEADLY SCORE: 25/30

WATCH OUT FOR THESE HIDDEN HORRORS!

STONEFISH

(Scientific name: Synanceia spp.)

Eats: fish and crustaceans

3

The most venomous fish on the planet, the stonefish is a master of disguise.

FEARSOME FACTS

There are several varieties of stonefish, with an average size of 40 centimetres (16 in). They are stocky fish with big heads and small eyes. They have warty grey-brown skin, sometimes with flaps and growths that resemble algae and help with camouflage.

GRISLY TACTICS

Stonefish have an amazing ability to look just like a rock or a lump of coral. They lie motionless and unseen on the seabed, waiting for their prey to approach, before lunging up at incredible speed to suck in their victim. The whole attack can last just 0.015 seconds.

KILLER FACT

STONEFISH CAN SURVIVE OUT OF WATER FOR UP TO TWENTY-FOUR HOURS.

AWESOME WEAPONS

The stonefish uses a deadly venom stored in its thirteen spines for defence. The venom is triggered by contact – most people are stung because they have unwittingly stood on the stonefish. The venom is potentially deadly and unbelievably painful, but luckily for humans there is an antidote.

STARGAZER

(Scientific name: Uranoscopus spp.)

Eats: fish and invertebrates

With its eyes fixed permanently looking upwards, nothing gets past this lightning-fast ambush hunter.

FEARSOME FACTS

There are around fifty species of stargazers measuring on average 18–25 centimetres (7–10 in) in length. They are dull brown, with large, flat heads, vertically slanted mouths and fringed lips. Their name comes from the fact that their eyes are on top of their heads.

DEADLY POINTS

FEARSOME FACTS:8/10

GRISLY TACTICS: 9/10

AWESOME WEAPONS: 9/10

DEADLY SCORE: 26/30

A TRULY SHOCKING FISH

GRISLY TACTICS

Stargazers bury themselves in the sand with only their eyes and mouth exposed, ready to leap upwards when prey approaches. Some species have a worm-shaped lure growing out of their lips which they wave around to attract other fish closer.

AWESOME WEAPONS

Stargazers have two large venomous spines that can cause pain and shock to attackers. Some species have organs placed behind their eyes that can deliver electric shocks of up to 50 volts, used to stun prey and for defence.

SOUTHERN BLUE-RINGED OCTOPUS

(Scientific name: Hapalochlaena maculosa)

Eats: small crabs, lobster and shrimp

Lurking in small cracks in reefs, this creature's size is tiny in comparison to the pain it can inflict.

Did you know?
The southern blue-ringed octopus is the most venomous mollusc in the world.

DEADLY POINTS

FEARSOME FACTS: 8/10

GRISLY TACTICS: 10/10

AWESOME WEAPONS: 9/10

DEADLY SCORE: 27/30

STAY AWAY FROM THIS TOXIC TERROR!

GRISLY TACTICS

The octopus inserts venom into its prey to paralyse it and then eats it with its sharp beak. It may also release a cloud of venom into the water and wait patiently for its victim to swim through it and become immobilized.

FEARSOME FACTS

The southern blue-ringed octopus measures up to 20 centimetres (8 in) and weighs a mere 26 grams (0.06 lbs). It has beige skin covered with brown patches – the vibrant blue rings are not seen unless the octopus is alarmed.

KILLER FACT

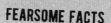

THERE IS ENOUGH VENOM IN ONE OCTOPUS TO KILL TEN HUMANS.

AWESOME WEAPONS

The blue rings on the octopus's legs are a warning to predators to stay away, but if that doesn't work, it will use its killer venom as defence. The bite of this octopus is painless, so victims may not realize they have been bitten until it's too late...

SPOT THE DIFFERENCE

Can you spot **SIX** differences between these pictures?

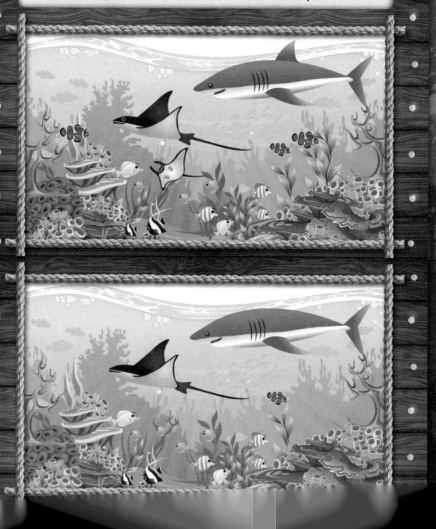

SEA MAZE

Show the shark the way to its snack!

Answers on page 74–75

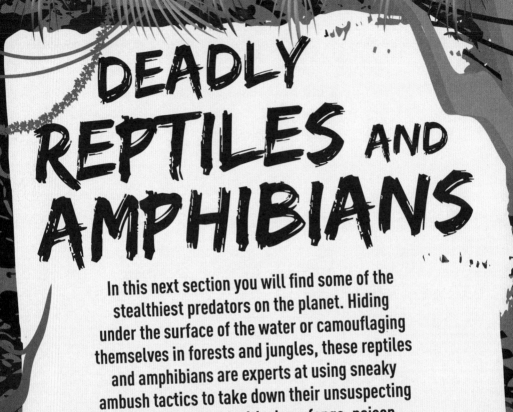

DEADLY REPTILES AND AMPHIBIANS

In this next section you will find some of the stealthiest predators on the planet. Hiding under the surface of the water or camouflaging themselves in forests and jungles, these reptiles and amphibians are experts at using sneaky ambush tactics to take down their unsuspecting victims. Equipped with sharp fangs, poison and killer teeth, there is no escape from these fearsome creatures!

SAW-SCALED VIPER

(Scientific name: *Echis carinatus*)

Eats: beetles, spiders, worms, frogs, small mammals and geckos

Also known as the carpet snake, the saw-scaled viper is the smallest of the deadly "Big Four" of Indian snakes.

FEARSOME FACTS

Saw-scaled vipers are relatively small, measuring between 50–70 centimetres (20–28 in) in length. They have pear-shaped heads with short, rounded snouts and large eyes. Their slender grey-brown bodies with white markings provide perfect camouflage.

GRISLY TACTICS

Saw-scaled snakes hunt by night and spend the day hiding. They threaten attackers by rubbing their scales together to make a rough, sizzling sound. This becomes louder and faster as the snake gets more agitated.

KILLER FACT

COILED LIKE A SPRING, THIS AGGRESSIVE PREDATOR HAS A SUPER-FAST STRIKE SPEED, AND AIMS TO BITE EACH TIME.

AWESOME WEAPONS

The lethal venom of the saw-scaled snake is kept in hollow fangs in its upper jaw. It causes bleeding, sickness and death in humans if not treated quickly. This snake is believed to be responsible for more human deaths than any other snake species.

DEADLY POINTS

FEARSOME FACTS: 4/10

GRISLY TACTICS: 5/10

AWESOME WEAPONS: 6/10

DEADLY SCORE: 15/30

SMALL BUT DEFINITELY DEADLY

BOOMSLANG SNAKE

(Scientific name: Dispholidus typus)

Eats: chameleons, lizards, birds and frogs

A shy, tree-dwelling and extremely dangerous snake native to sub-Saharan Africa.

DEADLY POINTS

FEARSOME FACTS: 4/10

GRISLY TACTICS: 6/10

AWESOME WEAPONS: 7/10

DEADLY SCORE: 17/30

A BEAUTIFULLY CAMOUFLAGED TREE SNAKE

FEARSOME FACTS

Boomslang snakes measure on average 1.4 metres (5 ft) in length and weigh around 3 kilograms (7 lbs). They have blunt, triangular heads with huge eyes, and three large, grooved fangs at the rear of their jaws. Females are brown, and males are often a bright pale green.

GRISLY TACTICS

Boomslangs are perfectly designed for hunting among the trees, with strong muscles and scales providing grip as they slide quickly along branches. Their excellent eyesight locates and locks on to prey, even if it is camouflaged. They move slowly towards their target before zooming in for the kill.

AWESOME WEAPONS

Boomslangs can open their mouths up to 170 degrees to deliver a paralysing venomous bite. Their extra-large fangs deliver a slow-acting venom that causes internal bleeding. When threatened, boomslangs inflate their necks to expose the bright colouring between their scales so they appear more intimidating.

DEADLY POINTS

FEARSOME FACTS: 5/10

GRISLY TACTICS: 5/10

AWESOME WEAPONS: 8/10

DEADLY SCORE: 18/30

A SPIKY-RIBBED POISONER

IBERIAN RIBBED NEWT

(Scientific name: Pleurodeles waltl)

Eats: tadpoles, small fish, worms and insects

A large newt with a uniquely weird defence mechanism.

FEARSOME FACTS

The largest European newt, the Iberian ribbed newt measures between 15–20 centimetres (6–8 in). It has a flat, spade-shaped head and a long tail. It spends most of its time in water although it can live on land.

GRISLY TACTICS

Iberian ribbed newts hunt in water and are voracious carnivores. They hunt by sight rather than smell so their prey needs to be moving for them to spot it. Newts have an amazing ability to regenerate lost limbs and other damaged body parts including eyes and even hearts!

AWESOME WEAPONS

This newt has a most bizarre method of defence – it forces its ribs through its skin to create a row of sharp points. At the same time it secretes a poisonous substance, so if any predator attempts to eat it the poison is injected into its mouth.

KILLER FACT

IBERIAN RIBBED NEWTS HAVE BEEN SENT INTO SPACE SEVERAL TIMES AS PART OF RESEARCH PROJECTS.

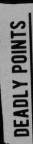

DEADLY POINTS

FEARSOME FACTS: 9/10

GRISLY TACTICS: 6/10

AWESOME WEAPONS: 4/10

DEADLY SCORE: 19/30

A SURVIVOR FROM THE AGE OF THE DINOSAURS

TUATARA

(Scientific name: Sphenodon punctatus)

Eats: crickets, earthworms, snails and lizards

A unique species found only in New Zealand, where it is the largest reptile.

FEARSOME FACTS

Tuataras were once thought to be lizards, but they are actually reptiles. They measure up to 60 centimetres (24 in) in length and weigh around 1.5 kilograms (3 lbs). Tuataras have a photosensitive "third eye" on the top of the head, used to sense light.

GRISLY TACTICS

Tuataras hunt by night. They have a unique teeth arrangement, with a double row of upper teeth between which they fit the lower teeth. They slice up their prey with a sawing motion, and bite the heads off birds.

KILLER FACT

TUATARAS ARE KNOWN AS "LIVING FOSSILS", AS THEIR SPECIES HAS BEEN AROUND FOR 200 MILLION YEARS.

AWESOME WEAPONS

Tuataras have the ability to break off their own tails when caught by a predator, and to regrow them later. They have a crest of spines running down their backs which can be fanned out when fighting. They grow slowly and can live to 100 years.

INLAND TAIPAN

(Scientific name: Oxyuranus microlepidotus)

Eats: rodents

Also known as the "fierce snake", the inland taipan is one of the deadliest snakes in the world.

FEARSOME FACTS

Inland taipans are large snakes, measuring around 1.8 metres (6 ft), although some can grow to 2.5 metres (8 ft). Their fangs measure around 5 millimetres (0.2 in). Inland taipans have dark tan skin, which they can change from light to dark in order to adapt to their surroundings.

GRISLY TACTICS

Taipans have good eyesight, and they use their forked tongues to detect the presence of prey. An extremely fast and agile snake, the inland taipan corners its prey before striking repeatedly with extreme accuracy. Its fast-acting venom instantly overpowers its victim.

KILLER FACT

THE SCIENTIFIC NAME OF THE INLAND TAIPAN MEANS "SMALL-SCALED SHARP TAIL".

AWESOME WEAPONS

The inland taipan has the most toxic venom of any snake in the world – fifty times more toxic than that of the king cobra. One bite can kill 100 grown men, 12,000 guinea pigs, or 250,000 mice! Taipans swallow their prey whole – enzymes in the venom help with digestion.

DEADLY POINTS

FEARSOME FACTS: 6/10

GRISLY TACTICS: 6/10

AWESOME WEAPONS: 8/10

DEADLY SCORE: 20/30

IT MAY BE SHY, BUT THIS IS A TOXIC KILLER

BLACK CAIMAN

(Scientific name: *Melanosuchus niger*)

Eats: rodents, particularly capybara, otters, fish and deer

A huge, underwater predator that lunges upwards to grab its prey unawares.

DEADLY POINTS

FEARSOME FACTS: 7/10

GRISLY TACTICS: 8/10

AWESOME WEAPONS: 7/10

DEADLY SCORE: 22/30

LARGEST PREDATOR IN THE AMAZON

FEARSOME FACTS

One of the largest alligator species in the world, the black caiman measures on average 5 metres (16 ft) in length and weighs 400 kilograms (882 lbs). It has a large head with a narrow snout and red-rimmed eyes set under a bony ridge.

KILLER FACT

CAIMANS HAVE BEEN KNOWN TO ATTACK PEOPLE, SOMETIMES FATALLY.

GRISLY TACTICS

Black caimans use their colouring to hide under the water. They snatch unwary animals drinking at the water's edge, and also venture into flooded wetlands to find prey such as deer and pigs. Their seventy large teeth are used for grabbing rather than chewing, and they swallow their prey whole.

AWESOME WEAPONS

The black caiman's sheer size and strength enable it to hunt a wide variety of prey. Caimans hunt by night, using their excellent hearing and eyesight. They have a third eyelid that they draw across their eyes to protect them while submerged.

DEADLY POINTS

FEARSOME FACTS: 7/10

GRISLY TACTICS: 8/10

AWESOME WEAPONS: 8/10

DEADLY SCORE: 23/30

A GIANT, POWERFUL LIZARD

KOMODO DRAGON

(Scientific name: Varanus komodoensis)

Eats: carrion, goats, water buffalo, deer and pigs

Apex predators in their environment, Komodo dragons will eat almost anything.

FEARSOME FACTS

Growing to 3 metres (10 ft) long and weighing over 150 kilograms (331 lbs), the Komodo dragon is the largest lizard on Earth. It has a stocky body with muscular legs and tail, sharp curved claws and a forked tongue for detecting prey.

GRISLY TACTICS

The Komodo dragon has large, curved teeth that can rip flesh apart. Lethal strains of bacteria and venom enter the wounds of its victim, causing blood loss and shock. Smaller prey is swallowed whole, while larger prey is left to die and eaten later.

AWESOME WEAPONS

The Komodo dragon waits until its prey is close before charging. With its powerful tail it can even knock down a water buffalo. Movable joints in its throat and neck allow it to swallow huge pieces of meat, and it can extend its stomach to consume more food.

KILLER FACT

WHEN THREATENED, KOMODO DRAGONS ARCH THEIR BACKS, LASH THEIR TAILS, OPEN THEIR MOUTHS WIDE AND HISS LOUDLY.

DEADLY POINTS

DEADLY POINTS

FEARSOME FACTS: 8/10

GRISLY TACTICS: 9/10

AWESOME WEAPONS: 8/10

DEADLY SCORE: 25/30

AN INCREDIBLY POWERFUL AND STEALTHY PREDATOR

GREEN ANACONDA

(Scientific name: Eunectes murinus)

Eats: fish, birds, mammals and other reptiles

One of the biggest snakes in the world, capable of eating prey as big as jaguars.

FEARSOME FACTS

Green anacondas measure up to 5 metres (16 ft) and weigh on average 227 kilograms (485 lbs), making them the heaviest snakes in the world. They are excellent swimmers and can reach speeds of 16 kilometres per hour (10 mph).

GRISLY TACTICS

The green anaconda lies submerged in water, waiting for prey to approach. It is a constrictor, overcoming its victim by coiling its powerful body around it and squeezing, or grabbing it with its teeth and dragging it into the water to drown.

KILLER FACT

GREEN ANACONDAS CAN GO FOR WEEKS OR MONTHS BETWEEN MEALS.

AWESOME WEAPONS

The eyes and nostrils of the anaconda are on the top of its head, allowing it to hide underwater to spot its prey. Its huge muscly body has stretchy jaw ligaments, so it can open its mouth really wide to swallow its prey whole.

KING COBRA

(Scientific name: Ophiophagus hannah)

Eats: mainly snakes, but also rodents and small birds

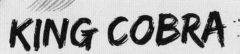

The world's longest venomous snake, king cobras are worthy of respect and fear.

FEARSOME FACTS

King cobras measure on average around 3.5 metres (11 ft) long but some can grow up to 5.5 metres (18 ft). Their deadly fangs are around 8–10 millimetres (0.3–0.4 in) long and are angled backwards to help swallow prey.

AWESOME WEAPONS

If attacked, king cobras raise a third of their bodyweight off the ground and flare their trademark hoods to make themselves look more intimidating. They hiss loudly before striking rapidly with their deadly venom-filled bite.

GRISLY TACTICS

King cobras use their forked tongues to pick up the scent of prey, and their keen eyesight to track it until the perfect moment to attack. They inject venom deep into their victim to immobilize it before opening their flexible jaws and swallowing it whole.

DEADLY POINTS

FEARSOME FACTS: 8/10

GRISLY TACTICS: 9/10

AWESOME WEAPONS: 9/10

DEADLY SCORE: 26/30

THE MAGNIFICENT KING OF SNAKES

KILLER FACT

ONE BITE FROM A KING COBRA CAN KILL AN ADULT ELEPHANT OR TWENTY PEOPLE.

SALTWATER CROCODILE

(Scientific name: Crocodylus porosus)   Eats: any animal that gets too close

The largest reptile in the world, the saltwater crocodile is also the most aggressive species of crocodile.

Did you know?

Saltwater crocodiles have the strongest bite force of any living animal, at over 16,000 newtons (a lion's is around 1,000).

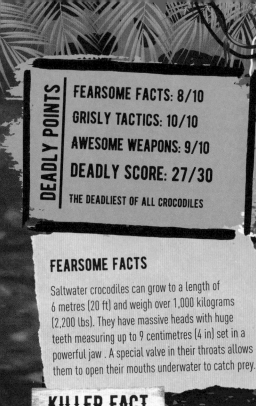

DEADLY POINTS

FEARSOME FACTS: 8/10

GRISLY TACTICS: 10/10

AWESOME WEAPONS: 9/10

DEADLY SCORE: 27/30

THE DEADLIEST OF ALL CROCODILES

FEARSOME FACTS

Saltwater crocodiles can grow to a length of 6 metres (20 ft) and weigh over 1,000 kilograms (2,200 lbs). They have massive heads with huge teeth measuring up to 9 centimetres (4 in) set in a powerful jaw . A special valve in their throats allows them to open their mouths underwater to catch prey.

GRISLY TACTICS

A formidable and stealthy predator, the saltwater crocodile swims silently up to its prey before striking at speed. It swallows smaller prey whole, and drags larger prey into the water to drown it before tearing off chunks of flesh during a "death roll".

KILLER FACT

THE SALTWATER CROCODILE IS THE MOST DANGEROUS CROCODILE TO HUMANS.

AWESOME WEAPONS

The sheer size of this crocodile means that it is capable of taking on any animal unfortunate enough to get too close to the water's edge. It uses its muscular tail to propel its entire body up and out of the water.

TRUE OR FALSE?

Can you say whether the statements below are true or false?

	TRUE	FALSE
1. Green anacondas are active hunters among the rainforest canopy.		
2. Male boomslang snakes are bright pale green.		
3. The Iberian ribbed newt can force its ribs through its skin to create a row of sharp points.		
4. Saltwater crocodiles only hunt prey smaller than themselves.		
5. King cobras have poor eyesight and only use their sense of smell to hunt.		
6. The Komodo dragon is the world's largest lizard.		
7. Inland taipans are non-venomous and kill their prey by suffocating it.		
8. Tuataras can break off their tails and regrow them later.		

DEADLY MATCH

Can you draw a line to match each fearsome reptile to its picture?

A. SALTWATER CROCODILE •

B. KOMODO DRAGON •

C. TUATARA •

D. BLACK CAIMAN •

E. BOOMSLANG SNAKE •

F. IBERIAN RIBBED NEWT •

Answers on page 75

DEADLY SPIDERS AND INSECTS

Small is definitely deadly! These tiny terrors have a huge variety of weapons that they use to hunt their prey. Here you will find spiders that shoot deadly sticky lines of silk and ones that hang upside down holding nets for unwary victims. This collection includes insects and arachnids loaded with venom, and the most dangerous ant in the world.

WHITE-TAILED SPIDER

(Scientific name: Lampona spp.)

Eats: other spiders

Commonly found in homes in Australia, these spiders go out hunting for prey rather than lurking in webs.

FEARSOME FACTS

Getting its name from the white colouration on the tip of its abdomen, the white-tailed spider has a grey body and orange and black banded legs. Females are up to 1.8 centimetres (0.7 in) long and males up to 1.2 centimetres (0.5 in).

DEADLY POINTS

FEARSOME FACTS: 4/10

GRISLY TACTICS: 5/10

AWESOME WEAPONS: 5/10

DEADLY SCORE: 14/30

A SPIDER THAT GIVES A NASTY BITE

KILLER FACT

WHITE-TAILED SPIDERS ARE OFTEN FOUND IN HOUSES HIDING BETWEEN SHEETS OR TOWELS!

GRISLY TACTICS

White-tailed spiders do not spin webs, they go out hunting at night, preying on other spiders such as the black house spider and the redback spider. They stalk their victims while they are in their own webs.

AWESOME WEAPONS

The bite of a white-tailed spider causes a burning pain, swelling and itchiness, and sometimes headaches and sickness. The bite leaves a red mark that can last for a week or more.

ASSASSIN BUG

(Scientific name: Reduviidae spp.)

Eats: other insects and mammal blood

9

An appropriately named insect that stabs its victims to death.

DEADLY POINTS

FEARSOME FACTS: 3/10

GRISLY TACTICS: 7/10

AWESOME WEAPONS: 7/10

DEADLY SCORE: 17/30

A TINY BUT DEADLY KILLER

FEARSOME FACTS

There are about 7,000 species of assassin bug measuring between 4–40 millimetres (0.2–1.6 in) in length. On average, they are at the larger end of this scale. One species can project its venom as far as 30 centimetres (12 in).

GRISLY TACTICS

Many assassin bugs are stealth hunters, approaching their prey slowly before attacking and stabbing it. Some are ambush hunters, lying in wait for their prey. Mainly these bugs attack insects, but some like to suck blood from vertebrates; including humans.

AWESOME WEAPONS

Assassin bugs inject venomous saliva into their prey through their beaks. The prey's insides are liquefied by the venom, and the body fluids can then be sucked up through the beak. The saliva can be used to kill prey much larger than the bug itself.

DEADLY POINTS

FEARSOME FACTS: 7/10

GRISLY TACTICS: 5/10

AWESOME WEAPONS: 6/10

DEADLY SCORE: 18/30

A SMALL SCORPION THAT PACKS A PUNCH

ARIZONA BARK SCORPION

(Scientific name: Centruroides sculpturatus)

Eats: insects, spiders and centipedes

The most dangerous scorpion in North America.

FEARSOME FACTS

Arizona bark scorpions have eight jointed legs and a pair of leg-like appendages called pedipalps which are used for sensing and grasping prey. They are around 5–7.6 centimetres (2–3 in) in length, with a segmented tail ending in a deadly stinger.

GRISLY TACTICS

These scorpions are stealthy and speedy nocturnal hunters. Nowhere is safe: as their name suggests, they can even climb trees. They can also crawl up walls and across the ceilings of houses, and are a threat to unwary homeowners.

AWESOME WEAPONS

The sting of an Arizona bark scorpion has been described as similar to being hit with a hammer. The extreme pain is followed by numbness as the potentially deadly venom begins to work, causing convulsions and loss of breath.

KILLER FACT

ARIZONA BARK SCORPIONS GLOW BRIGHT GREEN UNDER ULTRAVIOLET LIGHT.

OGRE-FACED SPIDER

(Scientific name: Deinopis spinosa)

Eats: beetles, ants, crickets and other spiders

7

DEADLY POINTS

FEARSOME FACTS: 6/10

GRISLY TACTICS: 7/10

AWESOME WEAPONS: 6/10

DEADLY SCORE: 19/30

A SPINDLY NET-THROWER

A goggle-eyed ambush hunter with an unusual way of capturing prey.

FEARSOME FACTS

Ogre-faced spiders have stick-like bodies around 2.5 centimetres (1 in) long with slender, spindly legs. Together with their brown colouring this helps them remain camouflaged during the daytime before venturing out at night.

GRISLY TACTICS

This spider has a unique way of hunting. It hangs upside down with a net suspended between its front legs. When its prey approaches, the spider propels itself downwards and entangles it in the net, wraps it up, paralyses it with its bite and then eats it.

AWESOME WEAPONS

Ogre-faced spiders have eight eyes like other spiders, but two of them are enlarged and are the largest eyes of any spider. They have huge, curved lenses and point forwards like binoculars, looking for prey. These eyes are specialized for night vision as they can gather light efficiently.

FAT-TAILED SCORPION

(Scientific name: *Androctonus* spp.)

Eats: crickets and other insects

6

Fat-tailed scorpions are found in deserts and are greatly feared by people.

FEARSOME FACTS

Fat-tailed scorpions grow to a length of around 10 centimetres (4 in) and are a brown-black colour. Their long, wide tails give them their name. They have eight legs and are arachnids, related to spiders.

DEADLY POINTS

FEARSOME FACTS: 6/10

GRISLY TACTICS: 7/10

AWESOME WEAPONS: 7/10

DEADLY SCORE: 20/30

ONE OF THE DEADLIEST SCORPIONS IN THE WORLD

KILLER FACT

THE SCIENTIFIC NAME "ANDROCTONUS" CAN BE TRANSLATED AS "MAN SLAYER" – ONE STING CAN KILL.

GRISLY TACTICS

Hunting by night, scorpions use their sharp pincers to catch prey before injecting it with venom to subdue it. They use sharp, claw-like structures in their mouths, called chelicerae, to pull off tiny pieces of food.

AWESOME WEAPONS

Fat-tailed scorpions have hard shells which provide defence against being eaten. Their main weapon is their tail, which can deliver venom as powerful as that of a cobra. The venom targets the nervous system, including the heart muscles.

BLACK WIDOW SPIDER

5

(Scientific name: *Latrodectus spp.*)

Eats: flies, beetles, caterpillars and mosquitoes

Feared around the world, this is a truly deadly spider with extra-potent venom.

DEADLY POINTS

FEARSOME FACTS: 7/10

GRISLY TACTICS: 7/10

AWESOME WEAPONS: 7/10

DEADLY SCORE: 21/30

A TINY SPIDER WITH A
FEARSOME REPUTATION

FEARSOME FACTS

Black widow spiders vary in size from 3–10 millimetres (0.1–0.4 in) in length. They are identified by the red hourglass markings on their abdomens. They have stiff hairs on one pair of legs, known as "comb feet", that are used to wrap their prey in silk.

KILLER FACT

BLACK WIDOWS GET THEIR NAME FROM THE FACT THAT SOME FEMALES
KILL AND EAT THE MALES AFTER MATING.

GRISLY TACTICS

The black widow spider lurks near the centre of its large web. It has poor eyesight and detects its prey by vibrations on the web. The spider rushes to seize its victim and cover it with silk. It then injects its venom into the prey to liquefy its insides.

AWESOME WEAPONS

The bite of the black widow contains a venom fifteen times deadlier than that of a rattlesnake. In humans, it causes extreme pain with muscle ache, sickness and breathing difficulties. Only the bite of the female is dangerous to humans.

DEADLY POINTS

FEARSOME FACTS: 6/10

GRISLY TACTICS: 9/10

AWESOME WEAPONS: 7/10

DEADLY SCORE: 22/30

A GIANT CENTIPEDE WITH A KILLER BITE

GIANT CENTIPEDE

(Scientific name: Scolopendra gigantea)

Eats: insects, spiders, rodents, bats and lizards

A giant creepy-crawly that is the stuff of nightmares.

FEARSOME FACTS

Giant centipedes can grow to a jaw-dropping 35 centimetres (14 in) long. They have up to 46 legs (23 pairs). On their heads are two antennae which they use to feel for prey, and they have two fangs, called mandibles, full of venom.

GRISLY TACTICS

These fierce creatures coil their bodies tightly around their victim while they deliver a venomous bite. When hunting bats, they hang upside down in a cave, with just a few legs clinging on, reaching out into the bats' flight path until they catch one.

AWESOME WEAPONS

The venom of the giant centipede is lethal for most small animals. Luckily it won't kill a human, although it can seriously wound, causing pain, swelling and fever. These fearsome hunters can run swiftly and also climb walls in search of prey.

SPITTING SPIDER

(Scientific name: Scytodes thoracica)

Eats: moths, flies and silverfish

DEADLY POINTS

FEARSOME FACTS: 8/10

GRISLY TACTICS: 8/10

AWESOME WEAPONS: 7/10

DEADLY SCORE: 23/30

A TINY ARACHNID WITH A UNIQUE HUNTING METHOD

A spider with a powerful spitting action that throws a deadly web around its prey.

GRISLY TACTICS

Spitting spiders tap their front legs to work out their striking range before spitting a sticky fluid from their fangs. It congeals on contact and traps their prey, after which the spider can wrap it in more silk. It then liquefies its victim's insides and sucks them out.

FEARSOME FACTS

Spitting spiders are tiny, measuring only 3–6 millimetres (0.1–0.2 in). They are orange with dark markings on their legs and body. Unlike most spiders they have six eyes rather than the usual eight.

KILLER FACT

SPITTING SPIDERS FIRE THEIR DEADLY SILK AT A SPEED OF 28 METRES (92 FT) PER SECOND.

AWESOME WEAPONS

The fluid that the spider spits contains a sticky liquid that it fires from alternate fangs, zig-zagging it across the target to form a net. The whole attack takes a mere 1/700th of a second. They also spit as a defence mechanism.

INDIAN RED SCORPION

(*Scientific name: Hottentotta tamulus*)

Eats: insects, spiders, lizards and other scorpions

The most lethal scorpion in the world, native to India, Pakistan and Nepal.

FEARSOME FACTS

Indian red scorpions measure between 5–9 centimetres (2–3.5 in). They range in colour from dark orange-red to dull brown, with grey spots on their head and back. They have brightly coloured legs and pincers, and a large stinger.

DEADLY POINTS

FEARSOME FACTS: 8/10

GRISLY TACTICS: 7/10

AWESOME WEAPONS: 9/10

DEADLY SCORE: 24/30

A BEAUTIFUL ORANGE-RED AMBUSH HUNTER

GRISLY TACTICS

Like other scorpions, the Indian red scorpion hunts by night, using delicate sensory hairs to detect the vibrations of its prey. It ambushes its prey, grabbing it with sharp pincers and holding it tight while it liquefies and eats it.

AWESOME WEAPONS

The venom of this scorpion is extremely dangerous, especially to children. Symptoms include severe pain, vomiting, breathing and heart problems, convulsions and death. Luckily, there is an antivenom treatment for those unfortunate enough to be stung.

Did you know?

Bulldog ants have six times as much venom as a honey bee, and have been known to kill an adult human within minutes.

FEARSOME FACTS: 9/10

GRISLY TACTICS: 9/10

AWESOME WEAPONS: 8/10

DEADLY SCORE: 26/30

FEROCIOUS JAWS AND A MASSIVE STING

BULLDOG ANT

(Scientific name: Myrmecia pyriformis)

Eats: nectar, plant juices, beetles, caterpillars and spiders

The most dangerous ant in the world, native to Australia.

FEARSOME FACTS

There are many species of bulldog ants, ranging in size from 8–40 millimetres (0.3–1.6 in). They weigh around 0.015 g (0.0005 oz). Some species, such as the jumping jack, can jump aggressively to warn intruders off, or to escape predation.

GRISLY TACTICS

Bulldog ants have carnivorous larvae, so the adults hunt to feed them, using their superior eyesight to track prey and dispatch it with a killer bite. They are aggressive and fearless, and fiercely defend their underground nests, stinging and biting any intruders.

KILLER FACT

SOME SPECIES HAVE NO WORKER ANTS. THE QUEEN RAIDS THE NEST OF ANOTHER SPECIES, KILLS THEIR QUEEN AND TAKES OVER.

AWESOME WEAPONS

The bulldog ant has long, toothed mandibles and a barbed sting, considered to be one of the most toxic in the insect world. The ant grabs hold of its victim with its mandibles, curls its body round it, and repeatedly stings it, injecting more venom each time.

TEST YOUR KNOWLEDGE!

Now that you've read all about these killer creepy crawlies, see if you can answer these questions:

1. Do white-tailed spiders spin webs? _____

2. Which is the most dangerous ant in the world? _____

3. How do ogre-faced spiders catch their prey?

_____

4. Which fearsome creature hangs upside down in caves to catch bats? _____

5. How many species of assassin bugs are there? _____

6. How many eyes does the spitting spider have? _____

7. What marking does the black widow spider have on its abdomen? _____

8. Which nocturnal hunter is often found lurking in homes in North America? _____

Can you fit these words into the spaces?
The first two have been done for you.

~~PREY~~　　　VENOM　　　STING　　　PINCERS

~~DEADLY~~　　　LARVAE　　　NEST　　　BITE

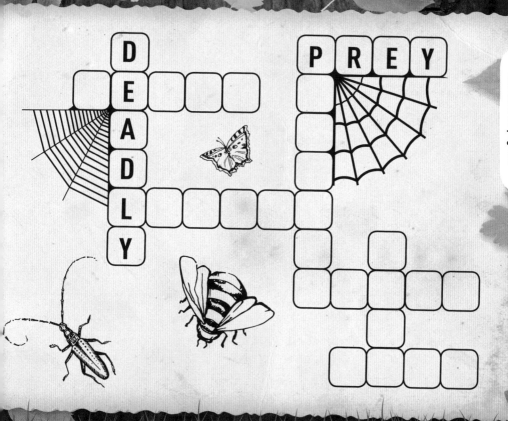

Answers on page 76

DEADLY WINGED CREATURES

From tiny flies and bees to giant birds and raptors, there are many creatures whose wings give them an edge when it comes to hunting, even if they can't actually fly! Some possess extra weapons such as venom or deadly parasitical saliva, while some use their massive wings to swoop down on their victims from the skies and snatch them up in sharp, deadly talons.

DEADLY POINTS

FEARSOME FACTS: 5/10

GRISLY TACTICS: 6/10

AWESOME WEAPONS: 7/10

DEADLY SCORE: 18/30

A SILENT NIGHT HUNTER

BARRED OWL

(Scientific name: Strix varia)

Eats: small mammals, birds, frogs and insects

A territorial and sometimes aggressive owl native to North America.

FEARSOME FACTS

Barred owls measure around 43–50 centimetres (17–20 in) in length, with a wingspan of 99–110 centimetres (39–43 in). They weigh between 500–1,050 grams (1.1–2.3 lbs). They are stocky brown and white birds with rounded heads and huge, dark brown-black eyes.

GRISLY TACTICS

Barred owls are territorial and will chase away intruders, hooting loudly, and sometimes striking them with their talons. They are even more aggressive during the nesting season. Barred owls compete with spotted owls and are thought to be responsible for their decline.

AWESOME WEAPONS

Barred owls are most active by night but also hunt in the day. Camouflaged by their brown markings, they watch from a perch before swooping down on their prey and grabbing it with sharp talons. They also hunt from the air, flying low through forests searching for small creatures on the ground below.

KILLER FACT

BARRED OWLS HAVE BEEN REPORTED TO ATTACK HIKERS.

RED-TAILED HAWK

(Scientific name: Buteo jamaicensis)
Eats: varied diet, including voles, rabbits, birds, reptiles, bats and frogs

DEADLY POINTS

FEARSOME FACTS: 6/10

GRISLY TACTICS: 7/10

AWESOME WEAPONS: 6/10

DEADLY SCORE: 19/30

A LARGE, SHARP-EYED RAPTOR

A common hawk that will attack almost any small animal it spots.

FEARSOME FACTS

Red-tailed hawks stand around 45–65 centimetres (18–26 in) tall, with wingspans of 0.9–1.1 metres (3–3.6 ft), and a weight of 0.7–1.4 kilograms (1.5–3 lbs). They have dark brown bodies with broad, rounded wings and a distinctive red tail that gives them their name.

GRISLY TACTICS

Red-tailed hawks watch for prey from a high vantage point before gliding steeply down to grab and crush it with powerful talons. Small prey is taken back to the perch or swallowed whole, and larger prey is ripped up and eaten on the ground.

AWESOME WEAPONS

The talons of the red-tailed hawk are relatively large for a hawk, with a rear talon measuring around 3 centimetres (1.2 in), enabling them to attack larger prey. They will aggressively defend their territories and chase off other hawks or eagles.

KILLER FACT

RED-TAILED HAWKS CAN EXCEED 190 KILOMETRES PER HOUR (120 MPH) WHEN DIVING.

MARTIAL EAGLE

(Scientific name: Polemaetus bellicosus)

Eats: varied diet, including bustards, poultry, antelope, monkeys, snakes and lizards

This mighty bird's scientific name, *bellicosus*, means "warlike".

FEARSOME FACTS

The martial eagle is the largest of the African eagles, measuring around 81 centimetres (32 in) in length, with an average wingspan of 2 metres (7 ft). It weighs between 3.5–6.5 kilograms (8–14 lbs). It has a dark brown back with a white belly and legs.

GRISLY TACTICS

Martial eagles mostly hunt from the air, swooping at great speed. They shoot their feet forwards and use their elongated hind claws to kill their prey. They also hunt from perches and may conceal themselves in trees or bushes near waterholes to ambush prey.

KILLER FACT

IT IS ESTIMATED THAT THERE IS ENOUGH POWER IN A MARTIAL EAGLE'S FOOT TO BREAK A MAN'S ARM.

AWESOME WEAPONS

With their keen eyesight, estimated to be over three times as good as that of humans, martial eagles can spot prey from 5–6 kilometres (3–4 miles) away. They can soar for hours, riding along rising air currents, and cover hundreds of kilometres searching for food.

DEADLY POINTS

FEARSOME FACTS: 6/10

GRISLY TACTICS: 6/10

AWESOME WEAPONS: 8/10

DEADLY SCORE: 20/30

A KILLER THAT SWOOPS FROM THE SKY

AFRICANIZED BEE

(Scientific name: Apis mellifera scutellata)

Eats: pollen and honey made from nectar

7

Known as "killer bees", these terrifying insects cause around forty human deaths in the US each year.

DEADLY POINTS

FEARSOME FACTS: 5/10

GRISLY TACTICS: 9/10

AWESOME WEAPONS: 7/10

DEADLY SCORE: 21/30

AGGRESSIVE DEFENDERS OF THEIR HOMES

FEARSOME FACTS

Worker bees are around 1–1.5 centimetres (0.4–0.6 in) in length, and queens around 1.8–2 centimetres (0.7–0.8 in). They are brown with black stripes and look similar to European bees. They build their hives in places like tree hollows, rotted logs and wood piles.

KILLER FACT

KILLER BEES WILL CHASE THEIR VICTIM FOR UP TO 1.5 KILOMETRES (1 MILE).

GRISLY TACTICS

Africanized honey bees attack to defend their hives and are particularly sensitive to the presence of humans. If they feel threatened, they swarm in huge numbers. Thousands can attack one victim, flying into ears, mouths, and eyes, and stinging again and again.

AWESOME WEAPONS

The venom of these bees is no worse than that of the European honey bee, but when so many sting at once it can be lethal. The bees release a pheromone if they feel threatened, which signals to the rest of the colony to join in the attack.

DEADLY POINTS

FEARSOME FACTS: 6/10

GRISLY TACTICS: 8/10

AWESOME WEAPONS: 8/10

DEADLY SCORE: 22/30

A SHAGGY-LOOKING AND SPEEDY BIRD

EMU

(Scientific name: Dromaius novaehollandiae)

Eats: seeds, leaves, grass shoots, plants, insects such as caterpillars, and lizards

The second-largest living bird after the ostrich, native to Australia.

FEARSOME FACTS

Emus can measure up to 1.9 metres (6 ft) tall and weigh between 18–60 kilograms (40–132 lbs). They are flightless birds but they have short, stumpy wings which they flap when running. Emus can reach speeds of 50 kilometres per hour (31 mph).

GRISLY TACTICS

Emus have immensely strong legs adapted for running fast and jumping high off the ground. They use their huge feet for kicking, and can rip the insides out of prey with their sharp claws. Emus are defensive of their young and hiss loudly to warn off intruders.

AWESOME WEAPONS

The unique structure of their brown-grey feathers helps emus regulate their temperature. They have an extra inner eyelid that protects their eyes from the dust. Their eyesight and hearing are excellent and help them to detect predators from afar.

TSETSE FLY

(Scientific name: Glossina spp.)
Eats: blood

DEADLY POINTS

FEARSOME FACTS: 8/10

GRISLY TACTICS: 7/10

AWESOME WEAPONS: 8/10

DEADLY SCORE: 23/30

A BLOODTHIRSTY AND POISONOUS INSECT

A deadly killer responsible for around 10,000 human deaths each year.

FEARSOME FACTS

There are around ten species of tsetse flies measuring 6–16 millimetres (0.2–0.6 in) long. They are dull brown in colour, and look similar to the common housefly. But they survive by feeding off the blood of other animals.

GRISLY TACTICS

Tsetse flies have a long, piercing proboscis which they use to chew through skin before sucking out blood. Their bite is extremely painful and can infect the victim with parasites which cause the human disease of African sleeping sickness, and the animal disease of nagana.

AWESOME WEAPONS

Parasites from the tsetse fly spread into its victim's bloodstream, causing fever, damage to the nervous system and even death. Cattle are often affected, and farmers in Africa have their livelihoods damaged by the loss of livestock.

KILLER FACT

EVEN THE LARVAE OF THESE FLIES PRODUCE A TOXIN STRONG ENOUGH TO KILL A HUMAN.

4

CALIFORNIAN CONDOR

(Scientific name: Gymnogyps californianus)

Eats: dead and rotting deer, cattle, sheep and rodents

One of the world's rarest birds, the Californian condor is so big that it looks like a small aeroplane!

FEARSOME FACTS

Californian condors are the largest birds of prey in North America, with a massive wingspan of around 2.7 metres (9 ft). They are 1.3–1.8 metres (4–6 ft) long and weigh between 7–10 kilograms (15–22 lbs). They are black with white patches under their wings and orange-pink heads.

GRISLY TACTICS

The heads of Californian condors are bald which helps them to stay clean as they stick them into rotting carcasses to feed. Their strong beaks can break the bones of animals such as goats, and rip through the tough hides of cattle.

KILLER FACT

CALIFORNIAN CONDORS CAN LIVE FOR UP TO 60 YEARS.

AWESOME WEAPONS

Californian condors have a poor sense of smell, but amazing eyesight which they use to spot prey from heights of 4,600 metres (15,000 ft). Soaring at speeds of 88 kilometres per hour (55 mph), they can travel up to 150 kilometres (93 miles) per day.

DEADLY POINTS

FEARSOME FACTS: 8/10

GRISLY TACTICS: 8/10

AWESOME WEAPONS: 9/10

DEADLY SCORE: 25/30

A MAGNIFICENT BUT ENDANGERED BIRD OF PREY

LAMMERGEIER
(BEARDED VULTURE)

(Scientific name: Gypaetus barbatus)

Eats: bone marrow from a variety of animals; tortoises

3

A majestic, mountain-dwelling bird with an unusual diet of bones.

FEARSOME FACTS

Lammergeiers measure 1.2 metres (4 ft) with wingspans of around 2.7 metres (9 ft) and a weight of 5–7 kilograms (11–15 lbs). They have long, narrow wings and a diamond-shaped tail. The bristles at the base of the beak give this bird the name of "bearded vulture".

KILLER FACT

LAMMERGEIERS LIKE EATING TORTOISES, AND DROP THEM FROM THE SKY TO CRACK THEIR SHELLS.

GRISLY TACTICS

Lammergeiers swoop down to scavenge bones, which they carry to a great height and drop on to rocks below to crack them open. More than other vultures, they hunt live prey too. Larger prey may be forced over the edge of cliffs to their deaths.

AWESOME WEAPONS

These vultures have huge, powerful wings to batter their prey to death. Their long, curved claws and strong feet help them rip through flesh to reach the bone marrow that comprises 85–90% of their diet. Their strong gastric fluids can easily digest bones.

DEADLY POINTS

FEARSOME FACTS: 10/10

GRISLY TACTICS: 10/10

AWESOME WEAPONS: 8/10

DEADLY SCORE: 28/30

NEST-RAIDERS WITH A NASTY STING IN THE TAIL

ASIAN HORNET

(Scientific name: Vespa velutina)

Eats: wide range of insects including crickets, flies and dragonflies

A fierce wasp that hunts and ambushes its prey and is a danger to bees.

FEARSOME FACTS

Asian hornets have larger heads in relation to their bodies than other wasps. They are dark, almost black, in colour, with a yellow-tipped abdomen and legs, and an orange face. Workers measure 2.5 centimetres (1 in) and queens up to 3 centimetres (1.2 in).

GRISLY TACTICS

These hornets are aggressive predators and hunt a wide range of insects. They also raid beehives using a technique called "hawking". Hovering outside the hive, they capture worker bees as they return from hunting, decapitate them and feed the protein-rich thoraxes to their young.

AWESOME WEAPONS

The sting of the Asian hornet is more painful than that of a honey bee, but the real danger is that of multiple stings which can trigger anaphylactic shock. Asian hornets will swarm and attack in great numbers if threatened, and some attacks have resulted in human fatalities.

KILLER FACT

ASIAN HORNETS ARRIVED IN EUROPE AFTER BEING ACCIDENTALLY IMPORTED WITH GOODS FROM CHINA.

AFRICAN CROWNED EAGLE

(Scientific name: Stephanoaetus coronatus)

Eats: monkeys, birds, antelope and lizards

The most powerful eagle in Africa, and an adept hunter among its native woodland and rainforests.

Did you know?

These eagles have earned the nickname of "leopard of the sky" due to their fearsome reputation as predators.

DEADLY POINTS

FEARSOME FACTS: 9/10

GRISLY TACTICS: 10/10

AWESOME WEAPONS: 10/10

DEADLY SCORE: 29/30

A FAST AND AGILE MASTER OF THE SKIES

GRISLY TACTICS

African crowned eagles can swoop after prey at speeds of 160 kilometres per hour (99 mph). When hunting monkeys, they often work in pairs, with one distracting the monkey while the other kills it, crushing its skull or breaking its back with powerful talons.

FEARSOME FACTS

African crowned eagles measure around 80–99 centimetres (31–39 in) in length, with a wingspan of 1.5–1.8 m (5–6 ft). They weigh up to 5 kilograms (11 lbs). They have a distinctive crested head that gives them their name.

AWESOME WEAPONS

Their grey colour, marked with black bars and blotches, helps these eagles blend into their forest habitats when ambushing prey. They have immensely strong legs and talons, and can kill animals weighing up to 20 kilograms (44 lbs) – that's four times their own weight!

KILLER FACT

THESE EAGLES ARE THE ONLY LIVING RAPTORS THAT HAVE BEEN KNOWN TO ATTACK HUMAN CHILDREN.

TRUE OR FALSE?

Can you say whether the statements below are true or false?

	TRUE	FALSE
1. Barred owls are aggressive during the nesting season.		
2. Red-tailed hawks will attack almost any small animal they spot.		
3. Asian hornets raid beehives so they can steal the honey.		
4. The martial eagle's scientific name means "warlike".		
5. Californian condors have a great sense of smell.		
6. The venom of the Africanized bee is ten times worse than that of the European bee.		
7. Tsetse flies cause a disease called African sleeping sickness.		
8. African crowned eagles work in pairs to hunt monkeys.		
9. Emus are the largest living bird on the planet.		
10. Lammergeiers drop bones from the sky to break them up.		

MAZE

Guide the eagle through the rainforest to catch the monkey.

Answers on page 76

ACTIVITY ANSWERS

PAGE 16

```
O C K V H I J O E B M O
X E O W U A Q N P C U C
W L N U O H I K L P I W
I E A Z U G R S Z G X I N
A B A R E A W A L A F H
S R R V U J R R J S O W
E X L R Y W P R X S J L
L O C H E E T A H O S L
W O O N I D Y X O F I J
Q U U U P O O O E H J L
U X K S F I E P D X O H
T M F S Q J Z A D A Y W
```

PAGE 17

1. B
2. C
3. A
4. B
5. C

PAGE 30

ACTIVITY ANSWERS

PAGE 31

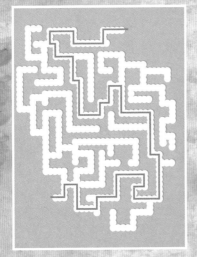

PAGE 44

1. **FALSE** – they lie in wait for prey under the water
2. **TRUE**
3. **TRUE**
4. **FALSE** – they can take on any prey due to their massive size
5. **FALSE** – they have excellent eyesight
6. **TRUE**
7. **FALSE** – they have the most toxic venom of any snake
8. **TRUE**

PAGE 45

A. SALTWATER CROCODILE •

B. KOMODO DRAGON •

C. TUATARA •

D. BLACK CAIMAN •

E. BOOMSLANG SNAKE •

F. IBERIAN RIBBED NEWT •

ACTIVITY ANSWERS

PAGE 58

1. No, they go out hunting.
2. The bulldog ant.
3. They hang upside down with a net suspended between their front legs.
4. The giant centipede.
5. 7,000
6. Six – most spiders have eight.
7. A red hourglass.
8. The Arizona bark scorpion.

PAGE 59

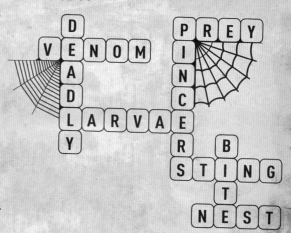

PAGE 72

1. **TRUE**
2. **TRUE**
3. **FALSE** – they capture the worker bees
4. **TRUE**
5. **FALSE** – they have a poor sense of smell but great sight
6. **FALSE** – it's the same
7. **TRUE**
8. **TRUE**
9. **FALSE** – it's the ostrich
10. **TRUE**

PAGE 73